THE WAY OF THE AMERICAN

ANDY HEATH

THE WAY OF THE AMERICAN

ONE

THE ANGER OF THE COMMON PEOPLE

The people are angry.

Very very angry.

We're often tempted to think we're angry at certain groups. Muslims and undocumented immigrants come to mind.

"They're taking our jobs!" or "They're going to blow us off the face of the Earth!"

Such tough talk is fun – for a while. We get to feel that anger and feel it deeply. We get to channel it in a way that provides a strong sense of cleansing, like if we can just get them back for all they've done to us, we'll feel better. And everything will be okay.

After all, our pain – that of the common people like you and me – is perfectly justified. If we look around and give an honest assessment of how things are going, we'll find there are many, many problems. We see a huge disparity of wealth between the rich and the poor. We see rampant racism, rampant sexism. We see white police officers murdering unarmed Blacks in cold blood. We see the wealthiest Americans getting everything, while we get nothing. We see the country's best healthcare going to those who don't deserve it, while we often have to beg. The hospitals and doctors send collection agencies after us.

We see our own loss of power over time. If we are religious, we see our religion persecuted. If we are this race or that, we see all the other races out to get us. Women feel persecuted by men. Men by women.

So how is it then that we live in the greatest country on Earth? Really, don't we live in the land of opportunity? Don't we live in a country that guarantees riches and the American dream to those who work really hard? And what of freedom of speech? Can we not express ourselves freely without fear of retaliation?

Do we dare, even for a moment, to think that maybe – just maybe – there's more to the story than what our 6th grade social studies teachers told us? Is it possible that we, a proud and common people, are actually getting the short end of the stick?

And perhaps more importantly, is it possible that there is something we can do that will actually make our lives in any way better?

Politicians will tell us that everyone should have the right to go to college, that everyone should have the right to an excellent job and high pay. But what about those of us who don't want to go to college or be a corporate executive or even an accountant or attorney? What of those who want to work in the "normal" jobs on which our economy depends? Do we not need people to take orders at fast food restaurants, to give basic care to the elderly, to clean the streets? Is there no dignity in such menial positions? What of those human beings, those who are perfectly happy doing such humble and important work and who simply want to make enough money to support their families without working more than one job?

There are answers to our problems, but we will not find those answers in the articulate speeches of our leaders. And we will certainly not find those answers in demonizing entire groups of people who have nothing to do with our suffering. Such is utter madness!

No, we will find our answers in kindness.

Of course, with those words, you'll immediately dismiss me as a weakling and a coward, but nothing could be further from the truth. Is it not a lack of kindness that creates all of our problems? After all, the reason Osama Bin Laden chose to attack the United States on 9/11 had nothing to do with our lack of ability to get revenge. We are a powerful nation, and he surely knew we would come after him and those who helped him if he were to undertake the grave attacks he launched on our beloved World Trade Center. It would have been much easier to bomb a country like Costa Rica, who doesn't even have a military. So why us?

And the answer comes in the fact that we have been unkind to others in the world. But as a proud people, we stood up after those attacks and "went after" the terrorists. They were trying to destroy us! At least, so said our leaders. The United States, minding its own business, was the victim of a vicious and absolutely unwarranted attack, according to our leaders.

If we were to say the attacks on our World Trade Center were our fault as the common people, we would also be wrong. The fact is, the common people had *nothing* to do with our lack of kindness to other nations, just as we have *nothing* to do with the vast majority of the foreign affairs our politicians undertake.

You see, our leaders in the past and present have created a culture of cruelty overseas. And our leaders are often as underhanded to the common people of other nations as they are to many of us. The common people overseas often lose their battles against us, and we only create more problems for them. Problems like poverty and oppression. We support "rebuilding" initiatives which only cause more problems than they were designed to solve. We give our own contractors lots of money to rebuild places like Iraq, and the common people there often reap none of the benefits.

Thus, the world's anger at us continues, and so do terrorist attacks.

But not knowing what to do, we see our golden opportunity at least to feel better, if not to protect ourselves. We see people in this country who do not look like us. We see Muslims – and wasn't it the Muslims who attacked us? We see undocumented immigrants – and isn't it they who take our jobs?

Of course, we the common people know in the deepest parts of our being that this is not true. But we're still swept away in the speeches of our politicians as they fight for the White House or whatever office they're interested in. We decide we need to go after the Muslims to make all our problems go away. We decide we need to oust the illegal immigrants to keep our jobs for our own. By God, we're America! We're powerful enough to do such things. We can wreak our own havoc on those we feel have hurt us. And by God, we'll feel better!

For a few minutes.

Then, if we're conscious enough as a society, we will see the serious nature of what we have done. We will see the cruelty we have inflicted on our fellow human beings who are guilty only of wanting exactly the same things we want. A house. A family. A car. A job. Enough money. Friends. Religion, in some instances. A creative outlet. Hobbies. A future for their children.

So you see, we look at these human beings, and what we see are others who are different. But in many ways they are simply not. They want all the same things we do. Yes, they often have a different culture or speak a different language. And we are certainly under no obligation to join them in those cultures and languages. But we can absolutely welcome them as brothers and sisters and fellow Americans. In that case, we will realize they're really not causing our problems.

So who is? Who is causing all the problems I've outlined in this chapter? This is an important question to answer moving forward, but first, we must look at the direction in which we're currently headed.

TWO

WHERE WE'RE HEADED

There was a man born in Austria in the late 19th Century, and he was a contemporary of Hitler's. He eventually wrote an autobiography, and I recently started reading it. This man, named Hans Schmidt, was a normal boy who went to school and studied. He enjoyed history and politics. He very much sympathized with his German heritage, and he saw the Austrian monarchy at the time as making an attempt to take away that heritage.

He remained on the back burner, however, because he had other outlets to pursue. He, like Hitler, enjoyed drawing. He painted as well, and he was also interested in architecture. But he was an excellent drawer, and his classmates and teachers told him so. He was going to go to an art institute in Vienna and study to be a great artist.

Around the same time, he took a history class taught by an instructor who had a great deal of influence on Schmidt. The young man loved history, and he came to enjoy politics, as well. His father, seeing promise in him, wanted him to go on to government service. Schmidt, however, had no desire for such a life, despite his interest in history and politics. No, he wanted the life of an artist – perhaps secondary to that, the life of an architect would have sufficed. But an artist he was determined to be.

He and his father often fought long into the night while his mother pretended nothing was going on. Schmidt honored his father and loved his mother. Still, he would never give in to such a dismal existence as that of a civil servant.

"I won't do it!" he shouted at his father.

"You will," his father responded, the anger in his eyes as clear as his resoluteness. But young Schmidt was just as stubborn as his father, and that was by his own admission in his autobiography.

Schmidt, though he would never do such a thing as to strike his father, raised his fist at the man.

"Not only will I not be a civil servant," he started, preparing to make a statement he might one day regret, "but I will not continue my studies. I'll go to classes, but I won't put forth any effort."

And so Schmidt was true to his word. He spent time practicing his drawing skills, but for years he and his father were barely on speaking terms. Schmidt never lost his warm affection for his father, but he steadfastly refused to allow that man to ruin his life.

Little did he know at the time that he would most certainly spend a career in government service, and that he would even seek out such a career.

Regardless, on the day of entrance exams at the Viennese art institute, he went in proud and strong. He had practiced and prepared for a long time. Everyone who knew him had flattered him and told him how amazing his drawings were. In fact, it never even occurred to him the review instructors wouldn't accept him.

But they didn't.

Furious, young Schmidt stormed into the institute director's office once he found out about his rejection and demanded to know why the institute hadn't accepted him. He was confused and angry. It seemed his life's dreams were dimming right before his very eyes.

"There's no mistake," the director informed Schmidt in a cool tone. "Under no circumstance will you be admitted."

"But this is all I've ever wanted to do," he responded, fighting back tears of rage.

"You might consider being an architect instead."

Schmidt stormed out the office. At first he was angry, but then he was just miserable. He spent his days working as a laborer, occasionally painting portraits, but he never forgot his failed dream of becoming an artist. So he became even more interested in politics. He frequently debated others, some of whom threatened him with physical violence for his fiery passions.

But threats like those didn't bother him. He was angry. Very very angry, like so many in his day. He faced constant poverty and hunger. His living quarters were horrendous. He saw no hope   not at first.

He looked to the movies and the theater he had so loved as a child, and it all seemed such garbage to him now. It was filled with people who had no talent. The material was garbage, trash, unfit to be seen. Perhaps it was his own sense of despair coupled with a rage of jealousy that caused him to feel that way, but that's exactly how he felt.

The arts were also filled with Jewish people, he noticed.

And he grew to hate these people, those who he felt had taken away his dream. These were the ones who were most fortunate. They had money. They had their careers. And it was they who caused his misery! He was sure of it!

Of course, by now you probably know that Hans Schmidt was not merely a contemporary of Hitler, but *was* Hitler. (My apologies for misleading you, but I wanted you to get through this last passage.) Hitler went on to become the dictator of Germany and made what some would argue a nearly successful attempt to take over the western world.

And how we despise Hitler now. How we *hate* him. He killed millions of people for no reason. We *should* hate him. Right?

Wouldn't it be nice if we could go back in time and somehow stop him from taking over Germany? We could have ensured his entrance into the art institute. We might have even killed him before he came to power.

But would that have done any good?

You see, Hitler himself was rather insignificant. He was actually just the natural result of a soil fertile for what he did. The fact is, whether it was Hitler or not, someone had to come to power and address the deep anger of the people at a moment of their economic despair. If Hitler had gotten into art school, he likely would *not* have had any interest in acquiring power for himself. Perhaps he wouldn't have hated Jewish people quite as much as he did. But do we honestly believe that *no one* would have come to power and committed such atrocities instead?

The Hitler phenomenon of World War II was bound to happen because the environment was ripe for it. The people were angry, just as they're now angry in the United States. It is possible that 50 or 100 years from now, the world might look back at us shaking its head and saying, "I just can't believe they did *that*." Whatever "that" happens to be.

We are currently a powerful country. We can discriminate against Muslims and undocumented residents of our nation if we want to. But will that do any good? Did it really do any good to discriminate against Jewish people in Germany during World War II? Just as Jewish people were not the cause of the German people's problems, neither are Muslims and undocumented residents the problem in ours.

Yes, we suffer poverty. We have a corrupt police force. A corrupt government. We languish under corrupt banks and corrupt billionaires who cruelly rule over us. We are a racist society. We are a classist society. We are an "us against them" society. And that will not change by building a wall at Mexico's border or keeping track of Muslims in this country.

Who, then, is the enemy? I would be tempted to say it's the CEOs who run large corporations and do unspeakable acts to harm others and enrich themselves. Certainly we could lash out against them, too. We could go with our torches and pitchforks and demand justice. But this, too, is frivolous action.

There is only one type of action more productive than competition, which is what we create when we lash out at others. And that's cooperation. If we take an enemy like poverty or injustice, we don't have to lash out against any group of humans. We can lash out instead against ideas that don't serve us.

There are those who say history is doomed to repeat itself. I reject that! While we have seen revolutions over the eons in which many people died at the hands of those who rose up to conquer their oppressors, this absolutely does not have to be the case. Just as Hitler did no good going after Jewish people during World War II, we will do no good attacking our Muslim and undocumented neighbors.

In order to improve our system, we must understand what is wrong with it. We must take an honest look at the real and painful problems with our broken infrastructure. Looking at these problems is not fun. It will not make us popular. We will turn our heads in shame at times and disgust at others. But we must see our injustice for what it really is. And we must define *true* justice. We must make a plan to achieve that justice, even if it means we do something different than we have ever done before in history.

Human beings are adaptable creatures. We have the capacity to learn if we will but bother to do so. Let's quickly explore the failures of our current system, along with a plan to correct those failures. In this way, we can move forward toward a more enlightened time in our history, whether we maintain anger at unpopular minority groups or not.

THREE

POLITICIANS DON'T HELP US

In our anger, we decide something must be done. We grow disillusioned with the leader we have had for four or eight years. We were not happy with George W. Bush, and many are not happy with Barack Obama. And these two are from different political parties!

"We must do something!" we cry out. Our anger only fuels us further. We then realize another election cycle is upon us. We listen attentively to the speeches the candidates make. First, we the people pit Republican against Republican and Democrat against Democrat. We watch as the candidates demolish and humiliate each other. The candidates themselves are broken after taking such abuse. The nomination winners going for the White House are so angry at the hell they have gone through, the true winner can barely catch his or her breath upon arriving at the steps.

Once we select the nominees after our process of holding state primaries and caucuses, the Republicans all become friends with each other again, as do the Democrats. Now they're vying for the prize, the presidency. They continue making their speeches and their promises. But now instead of attacking members of their own party, they join forces to attack the members of the other.

We the people watch this spectacle of cruelty and humiliation with ghoulish delight, while at the same time wondering which of these candidates will save us. "Bernie Sanders! Donald Trump! Hillary Clinton! Ted Cruz! One of these people will come to save us! They must! We can't take much more!"

And indeed we cannot. We listen to the debates, the speeches, the promises. We dare to hope things will get better. We want someone who will protect us from terrorists, make our lives somehow better, put more money in our pockets, keep our healthcare exactly the way we want it, create a society with a culture we can be proud of.

These candidates speak to our pain. They talk about all those who have hurt us or possibly hurt us. ISIS. Muslims. Gays. Terrorists. Undocumented residents. "We'll fix these problems!" they promise, licking their lips as they stand at their podiums. "We'll make everything okay. We'll make this country what you want it to be!" Then they look directly into the camera, their eyes smoldering as they try to hide their obvious lust for power. "Vote for me, and I'll make all your problems go away."

We don't really believe such promises, but we dare at least to hope. We want things to be okay for our future, for our children's future. We really *don't* like the groups the candidates speak against.

"We love the military!" they shout. "Those men and women in the Armed Services who risked or gave their lives to protect our freedom! We love Christians and working families. Only with God and with all of you can we move forward!"

We listen, and we continue trying to hope. We practically hold our breath as we hear the words of the candidates pouring over us, all promising a better future for Americans.

Then, what happens when these candidates get into office? Do they do the things they promised? Some of them, yes. They do some of them, but not all. After all, once they're in office, there is little anyone can do to remove them. We feel a sense of betrayal. These candidates once needed our votes, but when they finally get them, it seems they have once more abandoned us.

Now, instead of working to improve the lives of the common people, they are busy with wars overseas in places that really ought to be taking care of themselves (just as we ought to be taking care of ourselves). They spend their days and nights fighting with a childish Congress who simultaneously fights with each other.

Years pass, and they stand up to make their final speeches. They tell us all the things they have done to make our lives better. They talk about how they did this or that or passed such and such law. "The people are safer! More have healthcare! We ousted such and such dictator! *No* American is *ever* racist now that I have been president!"

And while some statements are true, others are absurd. Still, let's step back 100 feet and look at our lives after any president, especially George W. Bush and Barack Obama. Are our lives *really* better?

Do we have more money? Are banks less powerful? Are politicians more accountable and less corrupt? Do the wealthy no longer hide their money offshore to avoid paying taxes? Is healthcare really a reality for everyone? Are people really better off? Are they *really*?

The fact is, life is not better for the common people. It is worse. Politicians don't try to help us. They work to help themselves.

FOUR

AMERICAN EDUCATION

For years rest of the developed world has laughed at American education, but it is really no laughing matter. Let's start by looking at the wealthiest children from the most powerful families.

These children go to private schools. They are taught and trained to do well. Good grades mean you're a good person, as they tell their children. These children befriend each other, as do all children in schools across the world. Years later, they help each other when it comes time to get jobs and start businesses.

In public schools, especially in poverty-stricken areas, the children also befriend each other. The culture, however, is vastly different. Certainly there are some children who do well. They want to make good grades and go to college and live the American dream.

The wealthiest Americans, however, cringe at the very thought that Black or Hispanic or even poor white children would do well in school. The power of these wealthy Americans comes from the poor people's enslavement to a broken and unjust system. So these wealthy Americans are happy that poor and minority children frequently bully those who do well.

"We need to reform education so that no child is left behind!" cry the politicians. They stand with a smirk on their faces, knowing it's not true. But still, they know such statements are popular. They pass laws that teachers across the country have criticized, but were almost never consulted on, regarding how to help students.

Little talk is ever made of changing our culture, however. President Obama has spoken of it in at least one speech, but he's also done almost nothing to implement his ideas.

Children who do well in the public schools for low income children are often the targets of bullying so severe that psychological damage is inevitable. Eventually they hang their heads in shame from their abuse, and many of them give up. The bullies, ironically, are often even greater victims in these scenarios. They are the ones who don't do well at all, opting instead to put an inordinate amount of effort into social sports that, while fun, will almost certainly not provide them the opportunities to live a happy and productive life as an adult.

Years pass, and these children grow into adults. The new adults who went to private schools have the best opportunities for further education and lucrative work. The other young adults do not, and they must do their best, as poverty seems to be a curse passed from generation to generation.

I will point out, however, that the idea here is not that every student will do well in her classes. Some will, and some will not. It is an unpopular but true point that some children are simply not smart enough to do well. What of these children? Should they suffer?

The answer is clearly no. These children, once they grow into adulthood, should also have the opportunity to do well in life. They should receive wages that afford them a happy life with a family if they choose to have one. They should have access to healthcare and to education programs appropriate for their abilities.

In a successful society, everyone lives a life of dignity regardless of their performance in school. In a successful society, politicians care about everyone, regardless of their levels of education. Our society is not successful for this reason: Politicians don't care about us.

FIVE

SEX OFFENDER REGISTRY

We the people, in our anger, often have a keen thirst for revenge. So we will talk about one topic politicians avoid to any extent possible: the Sex Offender Registry.

Sex offenders are often sad human beings. They suffer the shame of their lives and seek to medicate that shame through sexual acting out that offends our sense of decency. They rape people and molest children. They are violent.

The question therefore arises – What do we do with such people?

Yes, they feel shame, and it is their shame and disappointment with their lives that often causes them to seek such thrills as sex offenses. So what do we do? As one of the most bone-headed ideas ever born in this country, we further fuel their shame.

We put them on the Sex Offender Registry and put their names online so people can go and see for themselves the humiliation in these offenders' eyes. In our cruelty, we gloat about how much better we are than such wretched people, may God have mercy on their pathetic souls!

Let's take a scenario though. Let's say you have five sex offenders, and let's say two of them are going to reoffend no matter what you do. One of them will not reoffend no matter what you do. Two of them are on the fence; they may or may not reoffend depending on a number of factors.

In the first instance, we put these five on the Sex Offender Registry. We abuse them and humiliate them. We make it easy to find them so others can torment and harass them. We assign them sadistic, power-hungry, childish probation officers who also abuse them. We make them live in certain places, often the least desirable venues to live.

In this scenario, we might see four sex offenders reoffend, as we didn't do anything at all to rehabilitate them.

In another scenario, we keep their criminal histories confidential. We do not post their information online or their pictures. We minimize the humiliation they have endured, as many of them are likely not happy to have committed such offenses. We give education and access to 12-step programs designed for those interested in controlling devious sexual desires. In this case, perhaps only two of the offenders would reoffend. That means, while we would still see some re-offense, we would see less of it.

We the people, however, cry for blood. We have no interest in protecting vulnerable people. We only want revenge on those who have committed terrible sex offenses. We want to make their lives as miserable as possible. We will resort to physical, social, and judicial violence if we must, but we the people will have our revenge.

Of course, this is madness. Sex offenders, like everyone else, are people. Those they hurt are also people. In maintaining the Sex Offender Registry, we bring further harm to both groups. It is madness, and it needs to stop.

This is an example where compassion would actually lower the rate of re-offense among convicted felons. True, it's not the kneejerk, emotional reaction we might crave, but it's a way that would work far better than the nonsense we are currently responding with.

SIX

CRIMINAL JUSTICE SYSTEM

Our judges are very smart, articulate people. When they sentence an African American man to eight years in prison for a drug offense, they can think of 100 reasons why it was justified. They can look at us, the common people, with their cool and condescending eyes and tell us everything they did to ensure justice.

However, if we step back 100 feet, we have to conclude it's simply not true. Black Americans receive harsher sentences than white Americans for the commission of the same crimes. Blacks and Hispanics are more likely to be arrested. They're more likely to be indicted. They're more likely to be sentenced. And they're *already* less likely to be hired for high paying jobs. Put that on top of a criminal conviction, and we see vulnerable minority groups remain in poverty and despair.

In this country, we have a Department of Justice, and we have judges who claim to support justice. But this is simply not true.

When judges make decisions, their own bias and rampant racism comes into play. They consult the laws, often written by blatantly racist legislators. They consult decisions that other courts have made, often by other racist judges. They hand out harsh sentences that have nothing to do with justice.

Ironically, those in our "justice system" never actually asks the question, *What is justice in this case?* They never simply look at the obvious factors that go into the makings of true justice. They are not even allowed to use their own brains to review a situation and point out the obvious.

For years, our leaders have said there is a problem with our racist justice system, but they have yet to make any real effort to reform it. The reason?

They don't want to.

They want to continue keeping Blacks and Hispanics down in this country so the white elite can hold on to its power. But when we realize that one out of every four Black male babies born today will be in jail at some point, it's just racist. It can't be anything else.

In my view, the criminal justice system is one entity that needs to be thrown out altogether so we can start over. Employers should also be unable to review a candidate's criminal history. Such reviews are pure madness and evil. If someone commits a felony, we should not intend to punish him or her for life. Yet these convicted human beings often find that life outside prison is even more difficult than life in prison, where they don't have to worry about money and shelter.

In this rare instance, I believe the best scenario is simply dismantling the criminal justice system altogether and starting over. We need to send criminal judges at all levels home. Yes, they should stop working as judges. There may be some who care and some who are not corrupt, but there are simply so many who are that they should all simply go home.

This seems a harsh thing to say, but it is true. We don't need to be angry at criminal judges or hate them, but we do need to send them home. They are simply acting contrary to the best interests of the common people. Those who ignore the interests of the common people need to go.

They need to leave the court houses and go home.

SEVEN

A BROKEN HEALTHCARE SYSTEM

Our healthcare system is so broken, I don't know where to start. We saw Barack Obama pass the Affordable Care Act, and we saw Congress try to destroy it. Why did they fight as much as they did? The fact is they fought because they were more concerned for their own individual interests than they were for the common people.

We can say a lot of things that will make ourselves feel good while making others very angry. We can say if people want healthcare they should get a fulltime job that offers it. We can say people should take better care of themselves. But if we step back 100 feet and look at our system, we can only conclude that it's broken and unfair.

There is simply no reason for a pill to cost as much as it often does. There is no reason for a hospital to charge what it does for its services. The only reason they have for this but will not tell us is that healthcare executives are greedy and they're preying on the masses who need them at a time of crisis.

And we frequently see human beings financially broken by one trip to the ER, a place where they often don't even receive the stabilizing treatment they're paying for.

Yet, these same people will argue that a government funded healthcare system would never work. They give their reasons, but these reasons make no sense in the face of reality. The fact is there are many countries who already have a government-funded healthcare system, and it works. It simply does.

The wealthy don't like such a system because their taxes would go up. They'd rather have their money than for us to have the care we need.

Changing over to a government healthcare system would certainly be painful for a while. Like any new system, it would have its problems. Those in the insurance industry might lose their jobs. Some people in our country might abuse the system. But these things are going to happen a lot of times anyway.

When we have a free market healthcare system, money comes first in a field where life and dignity should. People die unnecessarily every day because they can't pay for their healthcare. And when we pose this to insurance professionals or to the government, they often don't respond at all.

We would love to think the government cares about us and that they will take care of our healthcare, but this is simply not true. Our healthcare system is broken, and it will take a president more powerful than our childish Congress to fix it.

The idea here is that healthcare should be accessible to everyone, even those who have no money whatsoever.

EIGHT

WHAT WE NEED TO DO

May I offer a suggestion?

I'd like to be your president.

Of course, you laugh at a notion like that. After all, who am I to be your president? I have little money and less experience. Still, I would like to share a vision with you of what I think our country would be if I were your president.

I would make the poor wealthier. I would raise wages for all. I would make a life of dignity possible for everyone, even Blacks and Hispanics. Even those with little or no education. Even those who didn't want to work. Yes, even they would live with dignity.

I would dismantle insurance companies and give our government the responsibility of handling healthcare. I would ensure that everyone had access to whatever healthcare they needed, and taxes would pay for it. I would increase taxes for everyone, especially the wealthiest. But what we received in return would be worth it.

I would hold judges and police officers accountable for blatant racism. While I know well that racism would not end overnight, I would promote a culture of reward for merit, not race.

I would encourage our nation's children to love to learn so equality would be created for the future. I would consider eventually removing private schools from the mix altogether, so that all children of all backgrounds would connect, and we wouldn't see such rampant economic incest in our schools.

I would abolish the Sex Offender Registry, and we would see the number of sex offenses significantly decrease over time. I would also abolish Congress, as they largely act like children anyway and accomplish little. We don't need a Congress; we need a strong president who can run things correctly. Members of Congress would go home and get a job making a real contribution.

We the people do not have to repeat history. We don't have to go through the same painful lessons we have. But we *do* have to act.

Of course, I will never be your president. I don't have the temperament to lead you. I hope someone who does will stand up and take charge. I will gladly follow such a person.

We cannot ignore the fact, however, that we are angry. We have to acknowledge the fact that no politician in our current broken system will come to rescue us. We must rescue ourselves and take care of all people.

In doing so, we cannot lash out at other groups. This is what those in the past have done, but we cannot. We must practice kindness in our interactions with others, even if they practice a different religion, even if we have to send them home from their cushy government jobs.

But I leave you with this very simple truth: Our American government is beyond hope.

The only improvement we will make to the government is to abolish it It is time for the people, once more, to rise up as Americans did at the end of the 18th Century. We must take back our country and make it great ourselves. No politician from any background can do that for us.

Our government does not care for us. It is our greatest oppressor. It will not help us. They *all* need to go home. Presidents, legislators, judges, mayors, all of them. The leaders are simply not doing their jobs, and they need to go home.

In their place, we will install a sensible government that can bring about change quickly. Our currently government is too slow to reform. We need a leader who does not answer to a childish Congress. Right now the reason nothing can ever be done is the President and Congress are always fighting with each other.

We can put our hope in a politician if we want to, but it will do us no good. We don't need to elect any politician or businessman to the presidency. We need to end the presidency as it currently is and start all over.

We can certainly use the infrastructure that we have in place now – some of it, anyway. But corrupt leaders need to go home. It's as simple as that.

I will say it again. They need to go home.

May God bless America – and hopefully save her.

If you would like to discuss this work, you may email me at:

novelwriter@swissmail.org

Thank you.

Andy Heath

NOTES